"The Haunting One Silent Night"

By Patti " Sassy Angel" Chiappa

1

Dedication

This book is dedicated To my Husband Anthony who will always be my most blessed Christmas gift. Anthony to me you not only embody the true meaning of love but you share with me Heaven on earth. Your my soul's soul mate, your my irreplaceable shining star and the joy in my heart.

Acknowledgements

Frist of all, I would like to give proper respect to Mr. Charles Dickens who inspired many hearts by the original tale of Scrooge .The man who made me want to become a writer. I also want to send my love to my dad in Heaven. Every Christmas Eve ,my dad used to sit down and watch the movie with me. After the movie we share a cup of egg nog and talk about the meaning of this beloved tale. It was because of my dad that I keep Christmas well. To my dearest friend Gerry. Thanks for inspiring me to take a chance on rewriting an old classic. My dear friend Gerry is nothing like the Gerry in the first half of this novel. My friend Gerry's heart is bigger than St. Nick's himself. He loves humanity with a passion, and that is why I was inspired to write a new version of this beautiful old classic. If only people could love a fraction of how my friend Gerry loves the world would be a kinder , more gentle place. I would also like to send a big thanks to my mom and husband and nieces Kassidy and Jocelyn who are living breathing angels that embody the real meaning of Christmas. I would love to honor the shining stars on top of my heart's tree. My mother in law Roseanne and my father in law Anthony, Christen, Dale and Brian who always remind me that I am loved. To my dear friends around the world thank you for your support. To all those who share their love and talents, food, and gifts to those less fortunate. To all the Tiny Tim's around the world. Those children who never give up ,no matter what life throws at them. To my fans, this is for you. Merry Christmas! May you always find magic and the love of family and friends in this season of joy. To all those who keep Christmas in their hearts all year long. Unconditional Love is Divine Eternal Love: it endures despite all circumstances and it lasts forever. Thank you Mom, Anthony, Gerry and Stevi for your love. Thank you for being my four soul mates! I eternally love you. May you always keep Christmas well!

In His Grace,

Patricia" Sassyangel"Chiappa.

The Tiny Tim's of the world sing their praises……

"This is the perfect book for the holiday season. The simple message throughout this book will make your heart sing for joy."- Karen Whiteward- St. Luke's Catholic Church- Long Island, New York.

" Sweet, enduring and a great twist on the perfect classic."- Jim Brufast- Artist, Poet, teacher.

"Awesome. As a teacher I think my students will be able to relate more to this story then the original. Charming and Heartfelt."- Tara Westword.- Sacks Elementary School- Teaneck, New Jersey

" A great stocking stuffer for the book lover. All ages will love this book. "- Pastor Adrian Scott- Saving Grace Christian Church, Melbourne, Australia.

"Bravo, This tale is beautiful!"- Audrey Leudeman

" Uplifting and Unforgettable! A lovely tale that embraces the spirit of Christmas in a new and exciting way." Terry Bell

"Airport"

It was Christmas Eve. The fog at Heathrow Airport was at thick as pea soup. Gerry Cratchit , great grandson of Bob Cratchit sat inside the airport tunnel cursing the fog. " Bloody fog, sod off! I want to get back to the states!" The thirty-one year old with brown hair ,green eyes and a wicked smile that could break a woman's heart said.

A little boy who was about five years old pulled on the hem of his mum's wool skirt. "Mum, why is that man having a wobbler?" He asked. His mother looked at Gerry horrified. Soon the flight attendant from British Airways announced that all flights were cancelled due to fog.

Gerry ran a flustered thick hand through his thick and wavy hair. " Bugger!" He said balling up his fists. London was the last place Gerry wanted to be on Christmas Eve. Growing up in London, Gerry could not escape the legend of his great grandfather.

In Gerry's family's eyes , Gerry never measured up to Bob Cratchit ,the saint. So when Gerry was seventeen years old, he packed his bags and moved to America. It was there, before the Beatles ever set foot on American soil that Gerry made his small fortune. Managing the bank accounts for hippy rock stars. Gerry swore he never set foot in the United Kingdom again. He disowned his family.

But six months ago ,Gerry's parents passed away in a terrible tram car accident. It was then ,that his parents estate became Gerry's. Barrister Frances Scrooge, great grandnephew of the legendarily Ebenezer himself called Gerry with the horrible news. It took Gerry six months to care enough about settling the estate.

Frances and Gerry grew up together but were always great rivals. Frances like his great uncle kept Christmas alive in his heart all year long. Gerry on the other hand was like Ebenezer himself before he was visited by those three spirits that faithful Christmas night.

Gerry was not always a bitter, heartless and cold man. At one time he honored Christmas and loved the Lord. But something happened to change all that. A event that broke his heart forever.

"Bah Humbug!" Gerry complained as he gathered his suitcases. Gerry grabbed his designer suitcases. He then walked out of the airport into the cold night air. Gerry pulled his trench coat tighter around his body as his teeth chattered. Hailing a cab, Gerry did not head to a hotel but instead went to a local pub. As Gerry climbed into a hackney carriage, Gerry ordered the driver to take him to "The Mayflower Pub."

The historic pub dated back to the early 1860s. It was where the pilgrims gathered before they set sail to Plymouth Rock, Ma, Usa. The pub sits on a narrow cobblestone street. The two story building painted all white boasted flower boxes on the outside and oak beams, wooden paneling and real working fireplaces on the inside.

A crossed the street from the pub in a unmarked grave lied Captain Christopher Jones, the captain of the Mayflower.

Gerry threw a couple of extra pounds to the driver for the tip. Gerry grumbled as the driver wished him a "Merry Christmas."

Gerry grabbed his suitcase. He walked into the pub ,not looking at anyone directly in the eye. Gerry sat at the bar. A pretty young barmaid asked," What are you having?" Gerry replied ,"I will have a pint of Guiness and a cheese burger. Gerry was to wrapped up in his own problems to see a pretty young women walk into the pub wearing a wedding dress.

The vision in white dress was simple but elegant. It had a round neckline, sheer ¾ inch sleeves, empire line bodice that were smothered in cotton daisy lace ,white chiffon and white silk. Every eye in the house turned from the band to the crying and jilted bride .All expect Gerry's.

Tiffany Scrooge, The American great granddaughter of Ebenezer was 26 years old. She was striking beautiful. She had ocean blue eyes, long blond hair and creamy white skin that was soft to the touch. Tiffany always had a sense of adventure . At Twenty-one she was itching to explore the world.

So after Tiffany graduated college in New York with a master's degree in theater, Tiffany accepted a job in London. Tiffany had always dreamed of walking the same streets that her great grandfather walked on. When Tiffany got hired as the technical director of Rose Theater she thought her life couldn't get any better. But when Tiffany met Rufus King the great grandson of Benjamin Pollocks , the great toy maker she was swept off her feet.

Tiffany had only been in London for two days when Rufus helped her find her way around the strange city. On their first date Rufus planed a lovely candlelight dinner. That night Rufus and Tiffany talked for hours. Somehow by daybreak, they had fallen madly in love.

Over white pudding and coffee at a local eatery ,Rufus presented Tiffany with his grandmother's engagement ring. Tiffany accepted it. And This very Christmas Eve in front of her small, new group of friends, Sara a seamstress, Turner a lighting tech ,Sammy Tim an actress and Pastor Harry Marley Tiffany and Rufus were supposed to exchange nuptials in a romantic candlelight ceremony on Trafalgar Square. But instead of Tiffany's Prince Charming showing up on a white horse, Tiffany was abandoned at the alter in front of her new friends.

Tiffany bolted as fast as she cold from Trafalgar Square finding her way to The Mayflower Pub. It was there that Tiffany planned to abandon her troubles at the bottom of a pint. The Mayflower was so crowded that night with happy celebrators that it was almost standing room only.

Tiffany squeezed her way through the curious crowd . She made her way to the bar. Leaning over the bar to order her drink, Tiffany bumped into Gerry knocking his pint out of his hand and onto his shirt. " What an arse!" Gerry cursed. Gerry grabbed some napkins to try to dry himself off. " Oh God! A holiday maker dressed like an angel. Are you daft?" Gerry asked.

"Um, speak English please." Tiffany replied. " I am so browned off with this holiday!" Gerry said. " Look man! I didn't mean to spill your beer or whatever you people call it. Here let me buy you another one." Tiffany said in a cheeky tone. This had been the worst day of her life. Tiffany didn't need another nit wit in her life. "Don't bother to. I am clapped out anyway." Gerry announced.

"Huh? I really wish I could understand you, but I can't." Tiffany admitted. Suddenly Gerry realized that the women had no wings to her angel dress. "Hum, Where are your wings?" Gerry asked. Tiffany looked at Gerry like he had two heads. For the 1st time Tiffany noticed Gerry's dazzling eyes. Frowning Tiffany said ,"My wings?"

"Yes, you know angel wings. Aren't you supposed to be in a holiday play or something? I mean you are dressed as an angel." Gerry shared. With that Tiffany started to cry. "No! But I was supposed to be married today." Tiffany admitted. Gerry felt like a total jerk. "I should shut my bloody Gob." Gerry said as he handed Tiffany a tissues. "Thanks.", Tiffany said half-heartily as she dabbed her eyes. "Why don't I buy you a pint." Gerry suggested.

"I think I will pass. It was a bad idea for me to come here anyway. I mean I am just a stupid romantic who believed if I came to London, I find my fairy tale ending. I think I just going to go for a walk." Tiffany said. "You can't walk around London in your smart dress. Besides you will feel manky if you go out without a coat in this parky weather." Gerry replied. " Again, I don't understand a word you just said." Tiffany said. Gerry reached for his coat. " Here just take the bloody thing and understand what I am saying." Gerry said as cold as ice. Tiffany got up offended. " I don't need your coat! Ughhh! All men are creeps!" Tiffany yelled. The fire in Tiffany's voice stirred something in Gerry's steel heart.

He followed Tiffany outside the pub." I don't need a babysitter!" Tiffany screamed. " You are arseholed. I am sorry drunk. There's no way I am leaving you to wonder this city alone." Gerry said.

Sara turned on the lights in the beautiful Rose Theatre. The guardian angel found something magical about the old historic theatre that was built in 1587. Sara closed her eyes and pictured Shakespeare performing "Titus Andronicus." On the old historic stage. She could hear the clapping of the crowd. She could feel their joy. Sara felt the same feeling of joy when she danced for the first time in front of Jesus. Sara was so moved she began dancing.

Turner stood watching Sara for a few moments . She moved his soul. During the time Turner had been working with his fellow angel he developed a feeling of love for her. Sara looked breath-taking as she stood in the golden spotlight. When Sara opened her eyes, she was blimey to see Turner watching her. Sara's cheeks illumined with pink tint when she saw Turner smiling at her. " Oh, Turner I didn't see you standing there." Sara said shyly. "Sorry I didn't mean to startle you. I figured, I better check these spotlights straight away before tomorrow's performance of the Nutcracker." Turner dressed in grey pants and a green turtleneck replied.

" Don't you think we talk about our charges?" Sara asked a bit confused. " Actually Sara , we are on holiday. Our Heavenly father is taking care of this one. We are here just to give a gentle nudge every now and then. After all this is the most holiest of nights. Where anything is possible. This is the night hope outweighs fear. Strangers become family. Sadness is replaced with joy. Sorrow with laughter. This is the night that people hear the footsteps of their love ones in every heartbeat. This is the hour when people feel his breath and it becomes the oxygen they need to breathe. This is the moment That he whispers into lost souls with words of unconditional love ad understanding. Words so beautiful it leaves the lonely and forgotten drunk on hope. This is the moment where humanity hugs one another with its entire being. This is the hour warriors dissolve into the arms of peace. As dawn breaks this is the moment we are renewed in heart and spirit, hope and joy, forgiveness and possibilities.   This is the dawn we find ourselves in scared unity with love."

"Turner you just gave me Goosebumps. I never heard Christmas described like that before." Sara smiled. " More like God Bumps. He is after all the reason for the season." Turner replied. " I don't think Charles Dickens could have said it any better. It makes me sad through that on Dec. 26 , people will forget. The gift of music, the gift of God, Christmas Gifts, Birthday gifts. Yet one gift is irreplaceable, can't be reproduced , is one of a kind, completely divine . It is the most shiny, most bright, must lovely, must valuable and most loving. That gift was that Jesus died for us on a cross. His presence, essence and being the most beautiful gift ever born.   His light shines. He is the gift that loves, heals, helps, shows us to love, teaches us to forgive, and never changes. That is the gift that can't be wrapped. I wish on Dec 26 everyone could remember that." Sara wiped away a tear.

" I know I do to." Turner said as he placed a red filter into the spotlight. " Sometimes I wonder Turner if any of the work we are doing ever really leaves a lasting impression? I mean how many wars are being fought today? How many mothers will lose their babies to drugs in the gutter today? How many will go hungry tonight? How many lonely souls will cry out to be loved all on this Jesus's birthday?" Sara replied.

Turner walked over to his friend. Turner wrapped his arm around Sara. "It seems my little angel needs a faith lift." Turner remarked. Sara sighed. " Maybe even angels can become broken hearted and disenchanted seeing war, famine and people dying loveless day after day. The funny thing is all of God's children could help one another if they only took a moment to do so." "Come on Sara , let's go work on those costumes for the matinee." Turner said.

 Pastor Harry Marley, great grandnephew of   Jacob Marley stood in the vestibule of Westminster Abbey ,moonlight spilling in from the stain glass windows illumined his shadow. The fifty-four year old could not stop worrying about his friend Tiffany since she dashed away from the unhappy wedding scene. Candlelight from the holy candles flame flicked on the walls adding to both the serenity ,stillness and anticipation of that holy night.

Pastor Harry prayed as he sat down on the bench in front of the massive pipe organ. The Abbey was always a second home for Pastor Harry. The history of the Abbey spoke to his soul. The gothic statues, the resting place of Charles Dickens, Robert Browning and Sir Isaac Newton, the medieval coronation throne, stain glass windows always made   Harry remember no matter how much ugliness there was in the world, that if you search always find a bit of beauty also.

 Pastor Harry reflected on a scripture in Ecclesiastes 9:11   that read," I have seen something else under the sun. The race is not to the swift or the battle to the strong nor does food come to the wise or wealth to the brilliant or favor to the learned but time and chance happen to them all."

Pastor Harry looked up to a big and beautiful statue of an angel made out of solid gold. "Please protect Tiffany. Please make her see that all happy endings don't have to have a prince charming." Harry prayed softly.

"I told you I don't need a babysitter!" Tiffany scolded Gerry. "That is rubbish. You are so mug!" Gerry replied. As soon as Gerry said those words, Tiffany's high heal shoe got caught on a cobblestone sending her flying to the ground. Tiffany's panty hose ripped. Gerry bent down and picked her up. "See, I told you I couldn't leave you alone for one bloody second! Now belt up because I am not letting you go off on your own." Gerry replied. Gerry scooped Tiffany up into his arms. "Now are you going to tell me where you need to be or am I just going to be your horse all night?" Gerry said as ice cold as a snowman. "Fine! Just get me to the Rose Theater. I have some work to do there." Tiffany said. "Oh, so you are a spoiled actress." Gerry accused. "Put me down! I am not spoiled and I am not an actress! For your information I am the new Technical director." Tiffany snapped.

"Your ankle and knee are hurt, so I am not letting you walk on it. But if I am going to be your horse, I think I have earned the right to know your name." Gerry said shifting Tiffany in his arms. "My name is Tiffany, Tiffany Scrooge. And yes I am the great granddaughter of well you know. And what is your name?" Tiffany asked.

"Fish and Chips"

Gerry started laughing at that moment. The sound of Gerry's laughter surprised Tiffany because it was warm, tender and filled her whole being with a fluttering feeling. "It's not funny! Yes I am a relative of Scrooge, but so what?" Tiffany's anger amused Gerry. "Luv, I am not blast at that. I am the great grandson of Bob Cratchit. My name is Gerry." "Wait you can't be. I mean I heard stories that all of the Cratchit's died in a tram car accident." Tiffany said startled. "I am the bloke that the Cratchit family left out. I left for America at a young age. I haven't been back to London since. The Cratchit's and I only share one thing, our last name." Gerry shared as he started walking down the street.

Holding Tiffany over his shoulder with one hand and his suitcase in another. "Look I know I have spoiled your Christmas plans, but this has not been a good day for me either. Can we at least be civil to each other until you get me to The Rose?" Tiffany asked. "Yes, I am not a total wanker you know!" Gerry replied.

As Gerry walked, Tiffany got a whiff of his spicy aftershave .It was the same brand the man that left her at the alter wore. "I think ,I am going to be sick." Tiffany announced. Gerry abruptly stopped. "Don't get manky on me." Gerry said ,sitting Tiffany on a bus stop bench. "Did you eat anything before you started drinking like a fish?" Gerry asked in a cruel tone. " No!" Tiffany replied.

"Not to smart girl! Well do you think you can get some fish and chips into you?" Gerry asked. " Maybe some chips and Chi." Tiffany replied as she dry heaved. "Stay here ,I am going to get you something to wear. I have a mate that lives around the block." Gerry said. " And where do you suggest I change? In the motorway?" Tiffany sassed back. "Come on then, I haven't got all night." Gerry said.

Gerry carried Tiffany and his suitcase a crossed the street to a local dive. He knocked on the front door. An older women ,who was once a great jazz singer opened it. She turned as white as a ghost. "You wanker! I should make mincemeat out of you! You made me lose my life savings!" The women screamed. "Please that's all water under the bridge now. I need your help, actually she does. I was hoping you might have something for her to wear, and maybe some chi and chips?" Gerry said.

"You nasty ol' boy. You get your new bride drunk and then bring her here.!" The women dressed in a red gown said. Tiffany shared." Oh, no. I am not his bride. I was left at the altar, we are sorry to disturb you. It looks like you have plans. " Tiffany's face was drawn into a very tight frown.

" Oh, you poor dear. Please come in. My name is Bella." The older women said. Gerry harshly half threw Tiffany down in a chair. " Where's your loo?" Gerry asked Bella. Bella directed him to it. When Gerry left the room, Bella asked," How do you know Gerry?" Tiffany bit her bottom lip. Wiping a strand of her from her eyes, Tiffany replied," I don't know him, we just sort of ran into each other. Our families sort of know one another. My name is Tiffany. Tiffany Scrooge."

" Not in the great Ebenezer?" Bella asked. Wobbling her bottom lip Tiffany replied "Yes." Bella's face beamed. " Do you know that Bob and Ebenezer saved London town? After that faithful

Christmas night, Ebenezer was as good as gold keeping his word. He gave to the widowers and orphans. He befriended those in prison. He counseled the lost daughters of society. The biggest orphanage was built by Ebenezer and Bob. They laid the first bricks. The Hospital Tiny Tim recovered in was funded by the great and remarkable Ebenezer." Bella shared.

"I heard stories, beautiful ones about my great grandfather and the friendship forged between him and Bob. That's why I came here. I too want to make a difference. I don't know if I can do it on the large scale my great grandfather did, but I pray I can touch at least one life. After tonight however I don't think I will ever fulfil that dream. I thought I had found the love of my life. I thought my love had touched the deepest part of his being, but I was wrong." Tiffany started to cry.

Just then the room dropped 10 degrees when Gerry found his way back into the parlor. "What are you to hens gabbing about now?" Gerry asked. Bella put a pointed finger in Gerry's chest. " We are talking about maters of the heart. And seeing you don't have a heart, that's something you will never understand." Bella said. Bella then turned her focus back to Tiffany. "Can you walk Luv?" Bella asked. Tiffany tried to put some weight on her leg." Ouch," Tiffany said." It hurts."

Gerry rolled his eyes. " Here put your arm around me." Gerry said. Tiffany did. " Come , we will find something for you to wear, then I will get that cut on your knee cleaned up." Bella said. Gerry carried Tiffany into Bella's bedroom.

The bedroom was very small. It was filled with treasures form Bella's glory days. When Bella noticed Tiffany looking at a picture of her in her heyday, Bella said. " I was the headliner at the Dove Pub in the 1930 and early 40s. I was untouchable. I shined brighter than any star in the sky. Then I met a man. A man that stole my heart. We were madly in love. We had a huge wedding at the Abbey. We had a wonderful ten years together. When he became brown bread, I just feel to pieces. I couldn't sing. I drank like a fish. I became washed up. Then I met Gerry. He told me I was a gem. He said he would help me get my career back. If I could just invest a little bit of pounds. The market went bad and I lost everything."

"That's horrible! Didn't Gerry help you get your savings back? I mean didn't he offer you any help?" Tiffany asked. Bella avoided answering Tiffany's question by saying, " I should get you something to wear."

Sammy Tim, great grandniece of Tiny Tim, age 26 was Tiffany's best friend, actress, dancer, playwright, and good gal searched frantically all over London for Tiffany. The snow was coming down heavy and Sammy was freezing now. " Where are you Tiffany?" Sammy said to the cold night air. The air was so cold it hurt to breathe. With every breath that Sammy took more worry set in. Wide-eyed with fear Sammy searched all the places she thought Tiffany may have fled to. Sammy ended up right back at The Rose after hours of searching.

Sammy saw that the theater was empty expect for Sara and Turner. Sammy's heart sunk as Sara and Turner shared that there had been no signs of Tiffany. "Oh, mates what are we going to do? Tiffany does not know her way around London yet." Sammy said with a heavy heart. " Tiffany, it is in God's hands luv. Nothing is going to happen to her." Turner replied. " But we have so much work to do before the matinee tomorrow. No matter what Tiffany would have been here." Sammy said. " Why, don't you gals do a run through of the music. I think I am going to go out looking for Tiffany for a while." Turner suggested. " Maybe we should call a bobby?" Sammy said concerned. " I don't think we have gotten to that point yet. Tiffany has only been gone a few hours." Sara said. " I am sure we will find her." Turner replied.

" Are you two hens done yet? " Gerry asked. " Just about." Bella yelled out. " God, he is such a arse!" Bella said turning to Tiffany. " I don't understand what happened to him. He has the Cratchit's blood running through his veins. Why is he like that?" Tiffany voiced.

" I wish I knew. I have actually known Gerry for a while now and he has never opened up. He has a brick wall around his heart that no one can penetrate. Not even God. Luv, God has tried. God has sent his angels in the form of a lost puppy that Gerry once found. Gerry put the puppy down because the puppies cries annoyed him. Angels have come in the form of carolers ,that Gerry has sent away. They have come in the form of people wanting to be Gerry's faithful friend that he pushed away. It seems every year Gerry becomes more lost to humanity and more imprisoned by money and fame." Bella shared.

" The one thing that my family believes in is the miracle of Christmas. We believe that anyone is capable of change on this Holy Night. Even guys like Gerry." Tiffany smiled.

Gerry paced the small flat. " Bloody hell. Where is that woman!" Gerry said. Tiffany looked at the clock on Bella's wall. " Oh, I am so sorry. Here I am just chatting away and you have a party to go to. " Tiffany said. Bella's grey -blue eyes glazed over with sadness.   " It's a lie Hun. I don't have a party to go to. Oh, Bloody hell. Most of my friends are brown bread and the ones who are not are in rehab or to senile to remember me." Bella admitted. " Hey, I have an idea. I need to go to The Rose in a bit would you like to come with Gerry and I? I am the director of The Rose." Tiffany revealed.

" The Rose? I used to go there all the time with my Mum and Da when I was younger. My mum was a dancer and my Da was a piano player. It was my Da who gave me my love of music. Oh, you must think I am daft going on and on about this. The Rose is just a magical part of my childhood . All my treasured memories are wrapped within the walls of the Rose." Bella's eyes sudden sparkled with light.

Tiffany grabbed Bella's hand. Tiffany felt the paper-thin boney hand in hers and it made her smile. "Why don't you come celebrate with us at The Rose then? You know Bella this has not been a good Christmas so far for me, but meeting you tonight was one of the greatest gifts God could have given to me this year." " Oh, Luv you got me all chocked up. It would be my honor to spend my Christmas Eve at The Rose with you." Bella smiled. Tiffany's stomach rumbled then. " But first I am going to make some Chi and flapjacks for us." Bella smiled.

Not knowing what else to do with himself, Pastor Harry drove to the petrol station to fill up his red mini copper. He was praying he would spot Tiffany all the way to the station. " Father , please help your broken hearted daughter." Harry prayed.

" It's about time. Are you ready to go to The Rose?" Gerry asked as he struggled to try to pretend he didn't notice how stunning Tiffany looked. " Hold your horses chap. I am going to make Tiffany some Chi and flapjacks. And I suppose you will want some too?" Bella said. " You know Gerry, what this night is about? This night is about reflection. It's about looking at your life and finding the courage to look at yourself honestly in the mirror. It's about sitting still to take in the magic, wonder and beauty of this night. It's about finding peace in these moments of quiet. It's about forgiving yourself and the ones that hurt you. It's about finding new life in the baby's smile that lies in that manger. It is about the riches people find in all humanity on this Holy night." Tiffany shared.

" You know what I just heard? Blah, Blah, blah. I don't need you to preach the gospel of Scrooge and Bob because I have heard that preached all my life and it is rubbish. The thing I learned , the only real truth there is you have to take care of yourself. Cause others will always let you down. I say Bloody hell with humanity!" Gerry shouted.

Tiffany and Bella glanced at one another sadly. " How about some Christmas music?" Tiffany said walking over to Bella's radio with a limp. " Bloody hell, why don't you just put a bullet in my brain now?" Gerry complained. " Don't be such a Scrooge." Tiffany laughed. Bella looked at both Tiffany and Gerry. " You know you are the first company, I have had on Christmas Eve for 20 years. I think I am going to use the good china." Bella said.

Gerry rolled his eyes. " Can I help you with anything?" Tiffany asked. " No, you just sit there and enjoy the music." Bella replied. When Bing Crosby's White Christmas blasted through the speakers, Gerry's face became beat red. The anger in Gerry's voice shook Tiffany to her core. When Gerry got up and shut off the radio, shouting " Shut the blasted music off." Tiffany and Bella became very still. " This whole bloody holiday makes me ill. People pretending to care about one another. Peace on earth, yeah right. It's better to give then receive but yet shoppers will run you over to save a few pounds. All the false cheer , who needs it?" Gerry said.

"Gerry, do you know what you need? Some snaps." Bella said. " Now you are talking woman!" Gerry replied. " Flapjacks and Chi is ready dears. Here Tiffany you sit here. Gerry you sit right here next to her." Bella instructed. " Everything looks so festive and bright." Tiffany said. And it did.

The small oval table had a red table cloth on it. In the center of the table sat a precious candelabra with white candles that were lit. Bella had set the table with her best china. The dishes were silver and gold rimmed. The sliver once belonged to Bella's grandmother. " Everything smells divine." Tiffany commented, while Gerry sat stone faced. " Shall we say grace?" Bella asked. " Yes, please." Tiffany said. " Gerry , would you like to do the honors?" Bella asked. Gerry looked like he could actually punch a wall. " I will just take the snaps all right." Gerry replied.

Tiffany and Bella joined hands. Gerry however pulled away. Bella prayed," Dear Father. We come together on this beautiful and magical night not just as strangers but as friends. Remembering that the first gift of Christmas was the gift of love. As it says in Luke 2;19 " Many treasured up all these things and pounder them in their hearts." We two treasure up all these things, remembering, reflecting and pondering the baby in the manger in our hearts. Amen." " That was moving Bella. Thank you. Thank you for inviting me into your home. And for making the worst night of my life the best." Tiffany said.

Pastor Harry was horrified when he turned on his Telly to watch "It's a Wonderful Life." And instead a terrific and terrifying scene was unfolding on his black and white screen.

"Moonlight and Dreams"

Crying children, a devastated caregiver, fireman covered in ash, Bobbies trying to control on lookers and media. Smoke and flames everywhere.

Pastor Harry raced to the biggest orphanage in London. Volunteers from the Red Cross were trying to comfort the children. Pastor Harry ran around for the Bobby in charge. " Did all the children get out? Did anyone get hurt?" Pastor Harry asked the bobby nervously. " Everyone is safe. The children are heartbroken and scared but are safe. It's a miracle that no one got hurt." The bobby replied. " Do they know what started it?" Pastor Harry asked. " Electrical fire." The Bobby replied.

" So we have established you are an American, but where are you from?" Bella asked. Tiffany smiled brightly. " I grew up in New York City." " Oh, N.Y.C. that must be a fabulous place. I always wanted to visit there, but never got to go." Bella replied. " New York is magical at Christmas time Bella. New Yorkers stop and the city slows down. People even the most jaded become kinder. More sweeter. When that big tree in Rockefeller Center goes up all New Yorkers breathe a collective sigh of happiness. Our smiles become wider, our touch becomes a little more gentle and the world becomes a little bit closer." Tiffany shared having a dreamy look in her eyes.

"What rubbish! Pure Rubbish, at Christmas New Yorkers are more pusher, more greedier and more fast pace than ever!" Gerry growled. " Did they take lessons from you?" Tiffany fired back. " Are we about done here. I don't want to hang around you two hens all bloody night." Gerry said as wicked as a devil. " Uhm, yeah, I guess we can go to The Rose now. I will just let these dishes soak." Bella said. Tiffany jumped up from the table. With her hands on her hips, she shouted at Gerry." You are the rudest, meanest, cold-hearted man I have ever met. This wonderful woman has taken us into her home. Gave us a meal. And this is how you say thank you? If we wanted to be with a Grinch we would have called Dr. Seuss! You disgust me . I didn't think my Christmas could get an worse until now!" Tiffany screamed.

"You are a klaxon believing in the magic of Christmas. All that stuff about your great grandfather and my great grandfather is nothing but lies. All that about the three spirits or angels or whatever is all a made up fairytale by some desperate writer who met our great grandfathers a couple of times. The writer had a sick, romantic notion that some fairytale could change the world! But look around you. Are you blind? Are the poor and hungry still not found in dirty alleyways? Is there still wars among the lands? " Gerry questioned.

"You are wrong. What happened to my great grandfather was a Christmas miracle. A gift from God. A gift that changed millions of lives. If you just open your heart even for a second maybe you would feel the warmth of that Christmas miracle warm your soul. I don't know what has wounded you Gerry but we all have been wounded one time or another. Our scars do not have to define who we are." Tiffany said.

" Rubbish, all of it!" Gerry responded. Gerry grabbed his coat. As he did he stumbled backwards, almost landing in Bella's lap. "I am leaving. Pip, Pip Bella. Have a good life Tiffany." Gerry said as he walked out the door.

Tiffany felt a horrible sense of sadness as she watched Gerry walk down the footpath. Bella wrapped her arm around Tiffany's waist." I think we just met the real life Grinch." " We really should be going to the Rose, but do you think I should go after him?" Tiffany asked concerned. " Luv, Don't go chasing after any man." Bella replied." But he looks so sad." Tiffany replied. " Luv, Cinderella didn't go chasing her Prince charming, neither should you." Bella said." I guess you're right." Tiffany replied.

A woman from The Red Cross approached Pastor Harry with a dazed and sad look. " What is it?" Pastor Harry asked. " The children they refuse to be separated. No one wants to take 50 kids. I don't know what we are going to do." The worried woman said.

Pastor Harry paced and paced around the dismal scene. He tried to comfort all the children. Reassuring them everything would be all-right. One little girl with hair as curly as Shirley Templates, sad blue who escaped wearing just a thin pink nightgown and no shoes asked Pastor Harry," Where are we going to preform our Christmas play?" Pastor Harry knew the kids had been working hard for weeks to get ready for the highlight of their year.

Every Christmas day the kids would re-create the beautiful night that Scrooge discovered the true meaning of Christmas. Pastor Harry and the rest of the people who had ever seen the play were truly touched. How breath taking it was to see the poorest of the poor so rich with the Spirit of Christmas. Suddenly Pastor Harry had an idea. If only someone knew where Tiffany was!

Pastor Harry prayed that a guardian angel would direct Tiffany home. Harry needed her more than ever. Bella and Tiffany walked arm and arm to the bus stop. As they passed by a group of hippies, one man commented on how sexy they both looked. The man's comment made Bella as giddy as a school gal. It also made Bella realize that no matter how much older she got, she still was a knock out in God's eyes. " Bella, you are blushing." Tiffany teased. " That young lad reminded me I don't have to be taffee- nosed anymore. That it is alight for me to reach out to others." Bella replied.

" You shine bright beyond your imagination. You bless the world with your unmistakable presence. You inspire the hearts of those around you as you recognize your eternal essence. You change, bloom and grow and show the world that in love and with love things are not only possible but good. Celebrate your spirit everyday Bella because your beautiful. " Tiffany said.

The women chatted as they waited for the bus. Suddenly they heard a large and booming voice coming from behind them. " Are you two bloody hens still at it? Gossip, Gossip, Gossip!" Gerry said. " What are you doing here? You old Gaffer. " Bella said in an unfriendly and cold tone. Gerry frowned. " I am keeping you bloody hens safe. You would not make it to The Rose without me." Gerry shouted.

Tiffany decided she was going to use a different approach with Gerry. After all it was the season of good will. Tiffany's words dripped with sugar as she turned to Gerry saying" We would be honored if you would escort us to The Rose." " Don't mock me!" Gerry said. " Kindness in words create trust. Kindness in action creates peace. Kindness in giving creates love." Tiffany shared. Both Bella and Gerry rolled their eyes. Before anyone could say anything else the bus pulled up.

Bella and Tiffany sat together. Gerry sat in the back of the bus alone. Gerry was extremely annoyed with the Christmas music playing and the bus driver wearing a Santa hat. Bella and Tiffany chatted until suddenly the bus made an unexpected stop.

Fire trucks and blues and twos blocked the motorway. "I am sorry the constable's are not letting me through. We have to make a detour." The bus driver announced. Some people moaned but most people understood. Someone on the bus said ," Wait! Isn't the Children's home down the motorway?"

Bella got a horrified look on her face. Tiffany nearly passed out. Tiffany in a panicked voice said," Driver , I need to get off the bus Now!" "Miss , I can't let you off the bus it is to dangerous. "The driver replied. Tiffany walked up to the front of the bus with Bella and Gerry following. "You need to let me off the bus now." Tiffany said in a commanding tone. The bus driver looked bewildered. " Please let me off. I have a friend that works at the home." Tiffany explained. " All right you three only. Everyone else stays on the bus." The driver said. Tiffany ad Bella dashed off the bus. Gerry dashed off after them.

" Where are you two hens dashing off two? Are you daft? It is dangerous here." Gerry said. The women ignored him. Running full speed through puddles and over fire hoses, they finally reached the pitiful sight.

Pastor Harry stood in the middle of the scene looking lost, heartbroken and downright sad. His clothing was covered with ash and sot. Pastor Harry looked up at Tiffany with red and teary eyes. His bottom lip wobbled as Tiffany approached him. " Pastor did everyone get out safe?" Tiffany asked fighting back her own tears and fears. Pastor Harry could barely speak. He nodded his head "Yes."

 Bella running around like a chicken with no head, tended to the scared and small tots. Gerry without sheading a tear stood among the smodeling wood, burnt toys and lost dreams. Just looking as tough as ever said," Come on Hens, There is nothing we can do here. Nothing can be saved. "

Bella so distraught and angry with Gerry's comment, walked up to Gerry. Bella slapped Gerry a crossed the face. " How can you be so dead inside, that you can't shed one tear for these innocent babes who lost everything when they had nothing to begin with! How can you feel not even a drop of compassion?"" Bella shaking with fury asked Gerry.

 Gerry didn't even blink an eye when Bella slapped him. He stood there as strong as a stone wall. " Better these babes learn how cruel the world is, instead of living in a world of illusions. The children should know there is no season of hope, no generous angels that will fulfil their wishes. No fat man to bring gifts. Kids learn now that you can only count on yourself."

Suddenly as through he had fallen from the sky Barrister Frances Scrooge stood there in front of Gerry. " Gerry, mate why are you stepping on their hearts already broken ? Lift them up." Barrister Frances said. " Gerry shook his head replying," Why spin tales of happy endings when we know that's all rubbish?" " I am not going to stand here having an algy-bargy with you. I need to help these lads." Barrister Frances said.

Gerry stepped onto the sidewalk when he did he almost feel over a little lad about five years old. The little boy covered head to toe in ash was only wearing a pair of nickers and socks. He looked up at Gerry giving him the most painful look. "Mister, I don't believe in Santa. I asked him to bring me a mummy and Da and well he never does. I know he isn't real. Nobody loves kids like us."

Something in that little boy's truth spoke volumes to Gerry. Gerry grabbed a blanket that was being handed out by a foreman. He wrapped it around the little boy. In a cool and distant tone Gerry asked Barrister Frances ," Do they have a plan? I mean where are they going to house these kids?" Barrister Frances replied," What do you care?" Gerry looking down at his designer shoes mumbled," I-I was just wondering. That's all."

Barrister Frances posed a question to Gerry." What is Christmas Gerry?" Gerry without hesitation replied " For you bible lovers it's a time to shove your religion down our throat. "

" Your wrong Gerry. Christmas is Not about gifts, food, parties, Santa, Elves or even a mother or child in a manger. I think Christmas is a time to celebrate the family, friends and people that cross our path. It is a time to honor the spirit of hope, to practice the spirit of peace and humility. To allow ourselves if only for a moment to believe in the magic and beauty and the living love that shines in all of us. It is a time to embrace the world with our whole hearts. " Frances said.

Tiffany in an earshot said," He is right you know Gerry. Love is a perfume you cannot pour out onto others without getting a few drops on you yourself. So are you going to help us?" There was something in Tiffany's pleading eyes that opened Gerry's soul for just a moment. " Bloody hell, my night is already shot. So what is the plan?" Gerry said.

" We are going to move the children to The Rose." Tiffany shared." What? Are you mad? No one wants to come to The Rose tomorrow , paying good pounds to see the nutcracker and have a group of homeless kids hanging around." Gerry cruelty stated.

The same little girl that had approached Pastor Harry was in earshot. The small child looked up at Gerry. Her small cherub cheeks was full of tears." Mister, why do you hate us?" Gerry was speechless. " Hate? Dislike maybe but hate. The little girls eyes haunted Gerry. They were a mirror of how Gerry projected himself to the world. Not knowing how to answer the little girl, he said to the adults " Maybe it's not a bad idea." " Gerry, you can touch their faces and they might remember them for a few days. Or you can touch their souls and their hearts will never forget you. The choice is yours." Bella said.

" We should stop flapping our gums and get these kids into a warm place." Barrister Frances announced. "So how are we moving them?" Gerry asked. " They are NOT cattle!" Bella yelled. " All right." Gerry said disgusted. " It is freezing out here. Let's get the little ones to The Rose." Tiffany said. " How are we transporting the little ones?" Gerry asked his teeth chattering. " We have a bus standing by." Pastor Harry said. " I am freezing my duff off, so let's get the angels onto the bus." Tiffany said.

On the bus, Tiffany tried to keep everyone's spirits up by singing Christmas carols. Gerry refrained from commenting but felt sick. No one understood his pain. Suddenly when he glanced over to Tiffany, he noticed her hands were nearly frost bitten. Tiffany was sitting next to Gerry. Gerry grabbed Tiffany's small and soft hands. Tiffany wanted to jerk them back to her body, but the warmth from his breath felt good.

Gerry was surprised at how his insides turned to mush holding her hand. Tiffany herself was fighting off strange feelings. Feelings she never felt with Rufus. All of a sudden the heat between them made Gerry feel very uncomfortable. He dropped Tiffany's hands quickly. Tiffany tucked her hands under her legs, to keep them warm instead.

Gerry struggled to think of something to say to Tiffany. Not able to look directly at her , Gerry asked," So why did your groom stand you up?" " Why don't you just stick the knife into my heart a little deeper!" Tiffany snapped. Gerry took a white scarf and waved it. " I give up." He said. Something about the way Gerry waved that white flag, actually made Tiffany smile a little bit. " I didn't mean to sound like an arse. I was just wondering what happened between you." Gerry admitted. " I don't really know why. I guess maybe we rushed into it too fast. I guess we were thinking with our hearts and not our heads. I guess in the end it was to overwhelming for Rufus." Tiffany replied.

" Truce"

Gerry responded" Free soul, free heart, no bonds, no ties, no chains. That's the only way to live." Pastor Harry overhearing the conversation said," That's a sad existence son. I think the whole point of being alive is to love as many people as you can and to have a small impact on everyone you met."

"Friar, acts of virtue come from deep within, from the inter sanctuary of your soul. Where Inspiration flows. Every action has a seed in thought and every thought is a creation of a thinker , not of the soul. I choose what thoughts I want to create, what actions I make and what I want to experience in life. That pure love that lies in my heart is to make me happy no one else. Every thought I create is to benefit me and not humanity. We come into this world naked and alone and that's how we die. What happens between birth and death are solely up to that person. I choose to make myself happy and no one else because the truth is when you gasp your last breath it is the things you didn't do for yourself that you regret." Gerry proudly stated.

Tiffany turned to Gerry saying," This life is but a passing moment in God's eyes, but after we die is when we really start living. We can choose Gerry to live in paradise where eternal joy lives or we can choose to live in damnation. Every action we choose on earth either curses us or blesses us and that's the truth." Bella was blown away by Tiffany's phenomenal understanding of the life beyond this one. Bella said to Tiffany ," How are you so wise beyond your years? How do you have such a grasp on faith?" Tiffany replied," You don't grow up hearing stories of Scrooge and not be changed in some way." Everyone became quiet then even Gerry. Tiffany began witnessing right there on the bus. " All you have to do is open your heart to new possibilities and realize how much love is available to us. Don't you see God in these tots faces Gerry?" Tiffany asked.

Bella and Harry looked at one another , then at the scared children. They understood what Tiffany spoke of. Gerry however choose to stare at the back of the seat in front of his. " These children are God on earth and we are God's hands we need to shelter them." Pastor Harry said.

" That is so right." Tiffany agreed. " Oh, Please that's all rubbish." Gerry said." Whether you think it is right or not Gerry is your choice, but each of these little ones are a handprint of God." Tiffany said with her eyes overflowing with tears. " If you love kids so much, why don't you have a rug rat? " Gerry asked with disgust. With that question , Tiffany's hands went to her whom. " Are you duff?" Gerry asked. Bella was angry that Gerry asked Tiffany that. " Belt Up! That is that child's business not yours." Bella said. Tiffany turned to Gerry with tears in her eyes. " Oh, so you had to marry him! Your knocked up, that's why you rushed a wedding." Gerry smirked. " Your cruel! Crueler then a demon. I am not pregnant!" Tiffany said. " Oh sure you're not!" Gerry mocked.

Tiffany's eyes were puffy and red. " For your information, I can't carry a baby. When I was 14 , I was in a horror able car crash, and I lost all my reproductive organs! Are you happy now? " Bella said " Tiffany come sit with me." Tiffany squeezed her way past Gerry. When she got into the seat where Bella was sitting, she buried her head in Bella's chest and wept. " Are you happy now you dit?" Bella asked. Gerry replied," How was I to know?" His words put the blame on Tiffany. After Tiffany had a good long cry, Tiffany turned to Gerry. " Jealousy imprisons the spirit."

" Ha! Jealous? What do I have to be jealous about?" Gerry asked in a nasty tone. " Gerry, you are jealous of other's happiness . You are jealous of hope and love itself because you forgot had to love." Tiffany replied. " Look, you know nothing about me so don't pretend like you can gaze into my soul and understand my heart or any of my pain." Gerry said. " It's not rubbish Gerry. How am I able to wear a dress of purity and say I am done with the dark? How is it possible that this earth will always have daylight and no more night? Where does my heart exist without the journey between love and hate, joy and tears? It is God's path I walk over, it is God that marks my soul with beauty." Tiffany responded. Gerry was stunned silent. Tiffany knew she was touching Gerry's heart.

"My prayer for you today is that you will feel the spirit of Love wrapped in all the faces dwelling in all the places you may travel, visit, go. I pray you will feel the spirit of Love wrapped in frosty snowflakes, warming every breath you take filling your heart with peace. I pray you will feel the spirit of Love wrapped in your heart and your mind with you all the time through the seasons, years, right now. I pray you will feel the spirit of Love wrapped in everything, all things, living, loving YOU. You are the spirit of love. Open your heart, unwrap your joy, gift our world with your light. YOU are the spirit of love. YES! May you feel angel wings and sunbeam kisses warming your face this day. Happy people are not always the most thankful people but thankful people are always the most happiest. They are happy not because they have great wealth, power or fame but because the simple things within their lives hold greater wealth then the world could   ever hold for them. The more grateful of a person you allow yourself to be , the more love will come to you." Tiffany said.

Gerry got a thoughtful look of his face. " You poor Klaxon. You have been so brainwashed that you can't even think for yourself. I mean let's look at things. You are so blind. You gave your heart to someone freely, blindly and they broke it. Do you honestly tell me you would risk that kind of pain again? Where was your God to stop it?" Gerry asked.

Sammy sang her heart out as she gracefully danced. Sara smiled as she watched her. Sammy moved as through she had wings. It was as through, she was floating on a light summer breeze. Sara's breath was sucked from her lungs as sweet memories rushed through her mind. Turner stood watch over the weary firemen who were still trying to put out the stubborn fire.

Turner gave the firemen the extra strength they needed to fight the last wicked amber. Once the fire was completely put out , Turner returned to The Rose. Bella's eyes lit up as the bus pulled into the narrow parking lot of The Rose. Tears streamed down her face." The Rose, we are really here." Bella said. " Yes, Bella we are." Tiffany replied.

As soon as the bus came to a complete stop, Tiffany announced " I am going to pop inside and give others a heads up." Tiffany took long strides walking into The Rose. Sara looked up when she heard the front door squeak open. When Tiffany walked in, Sammy jumped off the stage. She tackled Tiffany like a linebacker with a strong loving hug. " Where have you been, we have been worried sick. " Sammy aske d in her thick accent. " I will tell you later, right now I need your help." Tiffany said. " Help?" Sara echoed. " Everyone got out, but the Children's home was burnt down to the ground. We brought the tots here , so we need all hands on deck." Tiffany quickly explained. " Sure what do you need us to do?" Sammy asked. The staff at the Rose made a plan. They set up cots in the lobby. Cots donated by the Red Cross. The women worked to get the wee ones to go to sleep. When Tiffany had a free moment she introduced Gerry and Bella to the rest of he r friends. Turner gave Gerry a hardy handshake. Gerry felt strange as Turner shook his hand. A feeling of light headiness came over Gerry. " Are you alright? You look pale." Tiffany said to Gerry. " It most have been those cheap booze and tasteless flapjacks I eat." Gerry responsed.

Before Tiffany could respond to Gerry's remark, a little girl screamed out, Don't hurt me!" " Who is that?" Gerry asked. " Her name is Miracle." Tiffany replied. " Well can't you shut her up? She will wake everyone up." Gerry said. " I'll attend to her." Pastor Harry said." Don't you care about anyone but yourself?" The little baby is dying. She cries out everynight because she suffers so!" Tiffany said. Gerry swallowed hard. " What's wrong with her?" Gerry asked in a small voice. "She has a very rare form of blood cancer. She thinks the boogie man gave it to her. That's why she is crying ," Don't hurt me!" Tiffany shared.

Gerry looked over at the scared little tot. Her lifeless eyes pouring with tears. Only a few strands of hair on her head. Her body shaking in Pastor Harry's arms. Something inside of Gerry's heart just broke. " I am not going to sit here all night listening to crying kids. I have much better things to do." Gerry said. Without saying another r word, Gerry walked out of the door into the cold and dark night.

" Someone should go after him." Barrister Frances said. No one made a move to do so however.

Gerry walked past the Mill bank Tower, Center Point and into the lobby of Trocadero Cinema were an old movie was supposed to be playing. A movie that had nothing to do with Christmas. Gerry paid for a ticket to see the movie

" Transform"

Gerry settled into a seat in the back of the darken cinema. A young couple in front of him eat popcorn. A older women looked like the only company she would have that day was of the strangers around her. Gerry's eyes turned from the crowd to the movie screen.   Gerry's eyes flew open when " A Wonderful Life." Began to play. " Blast!" Gerry said. " Shhhh!" Another person replied. Well at least Donna Reed was easy on the eyes Gerry thought.

Gerry shifted in his seat with the soda and popcorn he brought at the concession stand. It took all of Gerry's strength to watch the movie with empty arms and with her cheerful laughter. Gerry's heart cursed God for taking her away!

Gerry was haunted by the last poem Angel had written him. "Twas the night before Christmas and all through my heart, angels were busy doing their part To heal, inspire with presence Divine Reminding me, "Be still, This is God's time." For Love is the Source of all that is real Trust, for in faith, you will see clear. When outside the world clamors with chaos, Gunshots, violence, tears, such great loss, Staying centered, calm, hopeful can be A spiritual, human impossibility." Then deep from within me There came such a stirring My mind started reeling, My eyes went to blurring I yearned for joy to come somehow Heavily laden I cried; I wanted it now. In that moment the golden sun boldly arose And I remembered then what Love always knows. Love is the answer to every call. So let the light shine! Let light shine on us all. The light shines on you, dear friend. I send infinite blessings and eternal love to you this season. Angels abound! Only Love."

 Angel was nearly identical to Tiffany personally wise. She wa s full of life, passion, fire and dreams. Angel had a quick wit and a charming personally people were drawn to. Men flocked to her because e of he r green eyes, long   red hair and perfect figure.   When Gerry met angel he was not immune to her charm and beauty. Angel , a makeup artist and hairdresser for the stars was working in a salon on Fifth Ave in New York when Gerry walked in for a haircut. Angel was not impressed by Gerry's cocky personally or his looks. She had seen a million guys like Gerry before. When Gerry asked Angel to dinner, she laughed at him.   But Gerry as stubborn as a mule   worked to win her over. Gerry got a haircut every week until Angel would go out with him.

Gerry was only 19. Angel was 18.   Gerry took Angel to dinner and a Broadway show on their 1st date. On their second date in the early part of Summer 1959 , Gerry planned a picnic at Central Park.   This was the day Gerry knew he had found the second half of his heart.

 Gerry was so smitten, that he began to understand what his family had been trying to tell him all those years. That perfect love really did cast out fear. That Scrooge had experienced that perfectly heavenly love that   faithful Christmas night.

On Gerry and Angel's first Christmas together, Gerry hosted the perfect old fashion Christmas. Angel had never had that kind of Christmas because she had been raised in an abusive foster home. Gerry had picked out the perfect Christmas tree.   On Christmas Eve, Gerry cooked the most tasteful and traditional English dinner. A huge fat turkey, plum pudding, roast walnut stuffing and   fruit   cake for desert.

By the glow of a roaring stone fireplace, Gerry and Angel strung popcorn and decorated the tree. Dressed in their Sunday best, They attended a high Catholic mass as St. Patrick's. During that time, they were at mass all Gerry could think about was the black velvet box that was wrapped in red and gold paper sitting under the tee. A box that held an engagement ring. One that Gerry saved all year to buy.

As Angel belted out" It came upon a midnight clear" Gerry looked over at his Angel so overcome with emotion he cocked back tears. As they left church that night, a little snow blanketed the city streets making everything look like a magical fairyland. Gerry couldn't contain his excitement Christmas Day as he handed Angel the box. Getting down on one knee as Angel opened the box, Gerry said," My Angel will you make me the happiest bloke alive and marry me?"

Angel slipped the ring on her finger. She shouted " Yes!" After Gerry kissed her, he cried. Angel blushed as she usually did. Then a memory struck her." Oh, I forgotten your present at my place. If you finish setting the table, I will run home and get it." Gerry didn't think twice about Angel going back to her place because it was just around the block.

The last image Gerry ever saw of his beloved Angel was her twisted and mangled body under the car of a drunk driver. From Gerry's flat, Gerry could hear the glass shattering, People screaming" watch out." And Angel's screams. Gerry breathless raced down four flights of stairs to see the nightmare happening on the sidewalk. A doorman dressed in red desperately attempted to pull Angel out from underneath the car. Angel screamed with ever tug. Gerry pushed the doorman out of the way to hold Angel's hand and cradle her head. The only parts of her body that were visible to him. " Hold on baby. Help will be here soon." Gerry tearful said. On lookers wept , while others pinned down the drunk driver trying to flee the area.

" I am not going to make it Gerry. I love you." Angel gasped. As blood poured from every opening of her body. " Hold on, Please" Gerry begged. " Always remember Christmas was our day. Call me Mrs. Angel Cratchit just once." Was the last words Angel ever said.

Gerry kissed her blood and broken lips before she breathe her last breath." I love you Mrs. Angel Cratchit. " Gerry buried Angel in a lovely plot on New Year's Eve under a Christmas pine tree.

After Gerry lost Angel , he not only lost his faith in God but humanity. It took Gerry months to open his last gift from Angel. It was a handwritten book of poems , love poems for Gerry. Gerry's heart was torn up thinking about Angel and about how much she had wanted him to keep Her love of Christmas alive. Her legacy to the world.

Gerry ran straight out of the movie house crying. A young couple that passed him asked," Are you all right Bloke?" Gerry didn't look in their direction. Gerry so overcome, felt as through the pain was as new as the day Angel died. Like he was a madman, Gerry standing in front of Pollock's toy shop looked up to the sky shouting," Why God? Why did you take my Angel away? We were supposed to be married."

A group of party goers mocked Gerry's pain cruelly. Because they thought he was mad. Suddenly, Gerry noticed the light was still on in Pollock's. It dawned on Gerry then, Rufus must be inside. Gerry's pain turned into rage as he thought of the young and jittled bride Tiffany. Gerry looked through the window to see Rufus sitting at the work bench. A bottle of booze sitting next to him. Rufus eyes were blood shot. Rufus face was drawn into a tight frown. Something about the way Rufus looked, so broken, so lost, so sad brought Gerry to his knees. Gerry Remembered that look. Gerry felt drawn to help Rufus.

Gerry tried opening the front door of the shop but it was locked. Gerry knocked, Rufus would not answer. Gerry walked around to the back of the alleyway behind the store. He tried the back door. It was opened. Gerry walked inside the Toy Shop. He navigated his way through the crowded storage room. " Cheerio, Cheerio." Gerry called out. Only silence echoed back. " Hello." Gerry called out again. " We are closed!" A rough and drunk voice called back. Finally Gerry made his way to Rufus. " Bloody Hell. I said we are closed." Rufus said with fury., Rufus then got up.

Rufus very aggressively approached Gerry with balled up fists. Before Rufus could hit Gerry, Gerry said." I am a friend of Tiffany's." Rufus stopped dead in his tracks. " You must think I am scum. The biggest wanker on the face of this earth." Rufus said. " Um, You got that wrong. I am not here to judge. I just thought maybe you like to talk." Gerry replied. " Talk?" Rufus said. " I am pretty much having a bad night to." Gerry admitted. " How's Tiff?" Rufus asked. Gerry replied," As well as can be expected." " I love her you know." Rufus said. Gerry frowned.

" I know it's hard to believe but because I loved her so, I left her." Rufus said. " Love is not supposed to cause pain. Doesn't it say that somewhere in that bible you read? If you loved her then why did you abandon her?" Gerry asked confused. " I didn't want her to see me -" Rufus broke off his sentence.

Gerry laid a hand on Rufus's shoulder." You didn't want her to see you what?" Gerry asked. " I didn't want her to see me die." Rufus cried out. " Die. What do you mean?" Gerry asked getting chocked up. " I am dying Chap. It's my heart." Rufus sadly said. " How does walking away from the one person that loves you most in the world, help you or her?" Gerry asked. " Mush, have you ever seen a loved one die?" Rufus asked. Gerry walked away from Rufus. He walked over to the window.

Looking through the frosted window, Gerry answered," Actually I have. My fiancé. She was hit by a drunk driver. In front of my flat on Christmas Day. " " And how did seeing her die make things better?" How did seeing her take her last breath enrich her life?" Rufus asked. Gerry searched his soul for a long time. " I didn't know why until now, but I think I was chosen by God to be there in her dying moment." Gerry replied. " God, chose you for what? To watch your fiancé die, or to live in bitterness and pain? I know who you are. Everyone around her does." Rufus said bitterly.

" I was chosen to be a massager. A massager that hope still exists even in the most dismal of places. I was chosen to be a barer of joy. To show others what it means to smile while you are moving mountains. Rufus this is a mountain you are climbing and you don't have to climb it alone." Gerry said. " Your arseholed, look this has been hard enough on me, now I was going to give this letter to the posey but seeing your friends with Tiffany would you give it to her?" Rufus asked.

" So that's it? You're just going to leave   Tiffany alone and   with a broken heart? That woman , In the short   time I have known her she opened my eyes. My eyes to the truth, that God has not left us. That's   what this who night is about. God loving us so much   , he wanted to embrace humanity in a pure form as a child." Gerry said.

" Are you going to take the letter   Mate? " Rufus asked, still convinced he was doing the right thing.   " No mate, I am   not going to take that letter. I can't watch another woman die. You know   what I realized tonight mate? There are two kinds of death. Physical and   spiritual.   My fiancé suffered physical death but I suffered spiritual , that was until I met Tiffany." Gerry replied. Rufus got an odd look in his eye. " Do you think you can make her happy mate? I mean truly happy until she breathes her last?" Rufus asked.   Something in Rufus words   made Gerry understand that this was not just a question but a dying man's wish.

Gerry took a few steps backwards studying Rufus. " Are you asking me what you think you are asking me old chap? Gerry asked surprised. " I guess it depends on what you think I am asking." Rufus replied. " Sounds like you want me to be a   groom." Gerry admitted. " Well, you like her don't you?" Rufus asked as serious   as a heart attack.

 " For the couple of hours I have known her yes,   but I am not going to marry her!" Gerry objected. " But you do like her right?" Rufus said. " Chap, you must be feeling manky   because you are talking rubbish." Gerry responded.

" Downpour of Joy"

Rufus grabbed Gerry by his collar. " She's a good gal. I want her to be happy again. I want her not to be alone." Rufus eyes pleaded. " I understand but what I don't understand is how you can let her go so easy. "Gerry said. " Easy? Easy ? This is agonizing for me, but I have to let her go. Trust me this is not easy for me. But I have to let her move on. I only have two weeks if I am lucky." Rufus shared.

" I am sorry, very sorry." Gerry said compassionally. " That's life Chap, but I've had a good one. I don't regret anything. I don't regret meeting Tiffany or giving her up." Rufus shared. " Is there anything, I can do for you?" Gerry asked meekly. Rufus laid a hand on Gerry's shoulder. " Just take care of Tiffany please." Rufus begged. Gerry swallowed hard. " I will try." Gerry responded confused about his feeling for Tiffany.

Tiffany said," I sure wish we could give these tots a perfect Christmas." " Why can't we?" Sara asked. " How can we?" Bella wondered. " We have got plenty of food in our concession stands." Turner suggested. " Do you think we can pull this off?" Tiffany asked hopeful. " Of course we can!" Sara said her voice full of hope. " Let's do this for the kids and make this the best Christmas ever for them." Tiffany said.

Gerry walked out of Pollock's Toy Store with a large sack , a letter and a very confused heart. " The greatest power of all is the gift to love, why choose to be poor when love is abundant? " Was the last words Rufus said to Gerry, before handing a stack of toys to him.

When Gerry went to ask Rufus something after he started walking away, he was shocked to see a feeble old man sitting in Rufus place. " What's going on here. Where is Rufus?" Gerry asked. The old man looked at Gerry as through he had to heads.

" Rufus? Rufus became brown- bread early last night. What do you think I have been telling you." The old man said. " But he was just here." Gerry agured. The old man got up and smelled Gerry's breath. He cocked a half smile. The old Gaffer then said," Do you want me to call for a hackney carriage son?"

" I am not arseholed. Forget it gaffer. I am leaving!" Gerry said aggravated. As Gerry walked out of the Toy Shop feeling as though he was hit by a bolt of lightning. Gerry felt overwhelmed by emotions. Gerry walked down the footpath.

His skin bathe in golden starlight from a Christmas star. " Oh, God I am going mad." Gerry said to himself. Gerry kept walking down the footpath. Feeling like he was drowning under the weight of his emotions Gerry walked into the Abbey. He dropped the sack of toys by a statue of the Blessed Mother. Only the echo of Gerry's footsteps keeping him company as he walked down the center aisle of the church. Gerry took a deep breath.

He felt as though he was having a homecoming, a reunion of sorts with his maker. Gerry humblery and tearfully got down on his knees. So overcome with emotion he barely could talk. Gerry just kneeled at the foot of the large life like picture of the last supper.

But Gerry's eyes did not fall upon Jesus , they feel upon Judas Iscariot , the betrayer. Gerry looked into the uncompassionate eyes of Judas. It chilled Gerry to the bone, because he could have been looking into a mirror. Gerry realized at that moment, that he walked out on a group of homeless tots just as coldly as Judas kissed Jesus that night. Weeping , Gerry's tears had more weight with God then his words could have ever spoken. Gerry spent some very quiet time alone reuniting his soul with God. Gerry was taken back, when He heard a voice say," Welcome Home. From insurmountable obstacles facing you to overwhelming odds against you, Love is stronger than that. From chronic illness consuming you to the confusion and chaos swirling round you, Love is stronger than that. From the ghosts of the past haunting you to the phantoms of the future distracting you, Love is stronger that that. From financial worries to wounds and woes, from loss to doubt and even death. Love is stronger than that. Love is stronger than any of these. Love clears the path, lights the way, frees the heart and opens the mind to inspiration, action, hope and healing. Love is stronger than this world, stronger than your fears, because Love gives. YOU the strength to act on your own behalf. No matter how large your problems seem loom, Love is stronger than that. In you, through you, love is stronger than that. Today, if only for a moment, be still. Whatever you are facing, let love prove itself to you. Take action, follow intuition, feel better, stronger, free; then declare, "Fear, take that!" I see you inspired, taking a baby step, then running, dancing, celebrating, free! Yes , Love, my love Son is stronger then that." Gerry promised his maker he would return Christmas morning to celebrate his birthday.

" I sure we can find some gifts for the wee ones." Bella said. " I know, maybe we can raid the gift shop." Tiffany suggested. Turner who was aiding in preparing snacks for the tots said," I don't think we will need to raid the gift shop. I think Gerry will have a change of heart." " But where else will we get the tots some gifts? Gerry that selfish man will not come back." Tiffany asked sadden. "All the shops will be closed now." Bella added. Sara winking at Turner announced," We all need just to have a little faith."

Gerry knew after leaving the church, that his life would never be the same again. Before Gerry could take another step away from the church , Gerry finally found the words he wanted to speak. Looking up at Christmas star Gerry said," Your sweet serenity sooths my confused heart. Your white soft aura sways me so your eyes see right through my fears. I can hide nothing from your perfection. My head is bowed down before your grace. My soul is naked before your existence. You steel my breath with your grace and drown me in your love. Through my imperfections, my beauty still shines in your eyes. My humanity seems distant but now I am yours. Tears of joy fall from my eyes and you tilt my head up and with my smile I say ," I love you Jesus. Thank you for saving me this Holy night."

Gerry's heart felt lighter than it had been in years. His soul felt alive and happy. Gerry walked down the street, the sack of toys slung over his shoulder. His suitcase in his free hand. About four blocks away from the church, there was an open deli. Gerry got an idea.

Gerry walked into the deli with the sack and suitcase. A little old Italian woman and her husband was sitting behind the counter watching the telly. They watched in horror as a reporter stood in front of the burned out children's home. " I am sorry chap, we did not see you standing there." The older man said in broken English. The woman quickly turned off the telly. " May I help you?" The woman asked.

Gerry looked around the very small deli. Most of the cases were empty. " I will take whatever food you have left. All the kids form the children's home are staying at The Rose. I plan to give them the best Christmas ever. " Gerry explained. The older man looked lovingly at his wife. " The Rose, you say?" The old gaffer asked. " Yes." Gerry replied.   " Chap, we will deliver everything. You don't worry yourself lad. We will take care of it." The old woman said. " Thank you so much. What do I owe you?" Gerry asked.

" Nessuna, Carica. Merry Christmas.Il, Mio Amico. " The women said. Gerry who spoke a bit of Italian replied. "Grazie, per il bel regalo per I bambini." He then walked out of the deli with a huge smile on his face.

Gerry took a right on the corner and low and behold , there was a lot full of Christmas Firs! Gerry's heart skipped a beat as he marched up to the man selling the trees.   " Can you deliver?" Gerry asked the man. " Actually chap, I am clapped out and going home." The man replied. " Please this is not for me. It is for the tots who live in the children's home. It brunt to ground tonight. All the tots are staying at The Rose." Gerry explained. The man got a compassionate look on his face. " Why didn't you say so. I can make that my last delivery. Where do you want these trees delivered to?" The man asked. " The Rose." Gerry replied. Just then a Bobbie pulled into the tree sellers parking lot. " Hey, you old Gaffer, You with the red sack, come here." The Bobbie called out as he carefully walked up to Gerry. Gerry keeping his hands in plain sight asked," Is there something wrong?"

" Yes, something is wrong! How can you be St. Nick without a suit. My friends at the deli just told me what you were doing for the kids, now get in the car. The Chemist down the motorway has a suit you can borrow straight away." The Bobbie replied. Gerry smiled widely. He thanked the tree man. Gerry then gathered up his suitcase and the sack and got into the Bobbie's car with him. The heat blowing from the car vents felt good on Gerry's cold hands and feet.   The Bobbie studied Gerry for a moment.

" You are the Cratchit's kid aren't you?" The Bobbie asked. " Yes, I am." Gerry replied.   The Bobbie slammed on his brakes." You are the biggest wanker in all of London abandoning your Mum like that. She cried everyday for you. Your father walked around here like he lost his best friend. Get out of my car!" The Bobbie screamed.

Gerry tried to tell the Bobbie he was a changed man but it was of no use. Gerry defeated got out of the car, but not before the Bobbie gave him one more piece of his mind." " There is one word , that can change the whole world. That word is compassion. Learn it, use it, live it."

Gerry knew it was not the Bobbies fault for kicking him out of the car. He was only basing his option of Gerry on Gerry's reputation.   Gerry began walking as the Bobbie flew passed him as the smoke from the car's pipe mad e Gerry cough. Gerry came to the Chemist's office. Gerry peered through the front window. There wa s no sign of life inside.   With no luck, Gerry kept walking. Gerry began growing tried as he carried the heavy sack and suitcase.   When the first bus came along Gerry misread the sing in its front window to the destination the bus was heading.

He thought the bus was headed back towards The Rose but instead it was going to a place Gerry never wanted to see again. St. Pancras and Islington Cemetery , the oldest one in London. For Gerry it was the place his parents were laid to rest. The bus stopped right at the entrance of the cemetery. A few people got off the bus with Gerry. They were headed to a candlelight Christmas Eve vigil for their loved ones.

Gerry broke off from the group and through the knee-deep snow walked to his parent's grave. Gerry was utterly embarrassed when he looked at the cheap, small, cold barely visible headstone , he ordered for his parents grave. The plots around his parents all had big bright grave blankets and flowers . His parents grave had weeds and dead leaves. Gerry's guilt was eating him alive.

In the snow Gerry kneeled down. Starlight, moonlight and snowflakes landed upon Gerry's face and tear stained cheeks. " Mum and Da , I know I have been a huge wanker. I hurt you, abandon you, and with every fiber of my being fought against the legacy of Bob. I wish with all my heart, I could look into your eyes and tell you I am sorry. But I can't. What I can promise before God is that I will live out the res t of my days honoring the legacy of our family, loving others just as my great grandfather had.

Just as Gerry finished saying that, he saw something red in a nearby rubbish bin. Gerry puzzled walked over to the bin to investigate. My God, It was a brand new St. Nick suit. Gerry's eyes flew open. " Thank you Jesus!" Gerry proclaimed to the Heavens. Gerry dug out the suit. He gathered up the suitcase and sack. Finding a nearby Loo, Gerry tried on the suit. It was a perfect fit!

" Giving Grace"

Gerry walked out of the loo wearing the suit and carrying the sack and his suitcase. Suddenly Gerry heard someone whistling at him. " Hey St. Nick over here." A young man waving his arms wildly called. Gerry walked over to the young man who was actually a grave digger. " Bloke, you were not waiting for the bus were you? " The man asked. " I was." Gerry admitted. The man looked at Gerry puzzled. " You miss the last bus out of here a few moments ago." Gerry's frown returned.

The young guy jiggled the keys in his pocket. " You might have miss the bus, but you didn't miss the scooter. Do you know how to ride?' The young man asked. Gerry's smile became wide and bright. " oh yes of course." Gerry responded. The man tossed Gerry the keys. " It's the red one." The man said. " Thanks bloke, I will park it safely at The rose." Gerry responded.

The guy smiled at Gerry. When Gerry turned back to Thank the man , he was gone. Gerry was surprised when he found the red motorbike with ease. Gerry fir the suitcase and sack on the bike also. Gerry started up the bike and headed towards the Rose. The snow was really coming down heavy now. The streets were nearly deserted. Gerry felt at peace with God, himself and the world. Gerry took in the sites of his hometown. He was seeing everything with new eyes.

Gerry passed Harrods Dept. Store. The same store his parents took him to shop at when he wa s a child. Gerry smiled as he noticed the window display entitled " Oh , Holy Night." The window had a depiction of the 1st Christmas. A manger carved from wood. Hey, life-like donkeys and cattle statues surrounded the Holy family. An angel hovered over the scene. The thing that impressed Gerry the most wa s the star that made it come to life. It wa s something about that lonely and little star that made Gerry fully understand that it was ok to stand alone in this world as long as you were standing up for Christ.

" The Christmas Star.' Gerry thought had only one mission on that Christmas night to announce to the world the birth of its savor. Standing alone in the heavens illumined its light for all the world to see bravely. Gerry understood he needed to illumine his light for the world to see even if it meant standing alone and against all worldly desires and human wants. Gerry knew at that moment He would honor Rufus wishes and marry Tiffany.

" Tiffany, come straight away. There are Blokes outside coming to bring food for us and the tots." Sammy said. " I will be right there." Tiffany responded. Tiffany finished helping a little boy go back to sleep. She then walked over to the glass doors of The Rose.

She cracked it open just a hair." May I help you?" Tiffany asked. The older woman from the deli explained." The Cratchit boy sent us. We bring food for everyone and our friends from local pubs share it to." Tiffany smiled and said," Please come in."

Gerry was nearly at The Rose when he realized he had no gift for Tiffany. Gerry had a delmina. All the stores were now closed. Gerry stopped the motorbike in front of the lot were he found the Christmas trees. The lot was completely empty expect for a few broken branches, some pine cones and holly berries. Gerry was never good at arts and crafts, but somehow he thought maybe he could make a Christmas pin for Tiffany.

Gerry picked up some evergreen, a few berries and one pinecone. Gerry made a very small circle with the evergreen , making it look like a wreath. The pinecone wa s too big to use so he threw it away. Looking through his suitcase, Gerry found some superglue he kept for emergency. Gerry glued the holly berries on the evergreen. He added a pin from a sewing kit he had. He had mad e a pretty pin. He had no wrapping paper to wrap it, so he placed it in his suitcase . He was careful not to crush it.

Gerry then got back on the road, headed to The Rose. Gerry was in shock when he saw all the people at The Rose parking lot. There wa s delivery trucks, bags of toys, clothes and people helping people as though they were a family. Gerry stood stunned for a moment. It was a breath-taking sight.

Suddenly Tiffany came into the line of Gerry's sight. Tiffany let out a yawn, not knowing Gerry was watching her. In the moonlight Tiffany looked stunning. Her hair shimmered. Tiffany's smile illumined the night. Gerry had to catch his breath. He was nearly knocked off his feet by the spirit of love.

Gerry slowly got off the motorbike. Just as he did, Tiffany's eyes locked with his. Tiffany looked Gerry up and down and smiled wildy. " Well ,Ill be." Tiffany said grinning. Gerry took long strides at a swift pace to reach Tiffany.

When Gerry reached her, Gerry said," Love is the magic dust thet we sprinkle over any argy-bargy. It brings hearts healing, It guides us when we stand alone in the shadows of night. It makes our hearts sing when we have forgotten the words to our soul's song. It serves without wanting any thing in return. It turns the bitterness of the human heart into a joyful painting of grace. Love met me today. It came not in a shout but a whisper. Love did not condemn me for my mistakes but welcomed me home."

Ti ffany lifted her hand. She placed the soft palm of her hand on Gerry's forehead. " Nope, no fever." Tiffany said half laughing. " im serious." Gerry said. " Do you want to know my weakness Gerry? My weakness is I see the good in everyone. And the man standing before me, all I can see is good. Now I know you see it also." Tiffany replied.

Gerry looked down at his feet. He was not yet ready to share his feelings of his heart with Tiffany. So he changed the subject. " So who are all these people?" Tiffany laced her arm through Gerry's. " Come on St. Nick you have some little ones to see." Gerry laughed saying " I am starving is there anything to eat?"

Tiffany rolled her eyes." We have bread and water." Gerry and Tiffany walked into The Rose arm and arm. Gerry was touched by what he saw unfolding inside. A group of youngers , along with Barrister Frances wa s decorating a Christmas Fir. Younger tots were decorating with paper decorations with Sammy. Another group were eating deli food that Pastor Harry was passing out. Gerry watched as Bella set up a radio that blasted out carols. Everyone was so busy they did not notice Gerry or Tiffany.

A little tot eating Christmas candy was the 1st to notice Gerry. " Santa! Santa ! You came!" The restless little boy shouted as he ran towards Gerry. Gerry dropped the sack. He caught the little boy in his arms. " I love you Santa." The little boy tearfully said as through he just met his best friend. " Ho, Ho, Ho, I love you also." Gerry replied in his best Santa voice.

All the little ones made a bee line towards Gerry. " Santa, How did you find us?" Asked one little girl. Gerry pitched the little girl's cheek. " I always know where you are." Gerry said smiling. All the tots started laughing. The adults too. " Santa this is the best night of my life. Before you came my faith was bone idle but with you here, the fire in my belly is renewed." Tiffany said.

The little girl that was sick, pulled on Gerry's hand. Gerry lifted he r into his arms. " Hello, wee one." Gerry said in a jolly voice. The little girl with the angelic face stopped all the fest ivies with her soft question. " Do you know God Santa?" She asked. Gerry felt tears welling up in his eyes. He did nothing to hid e them. " Yes, wee one. I do." Gerry responded whole-heartily. " Does that mean when I go to Heaven , you will still bring me a Christmas Gift?" The little babe asked.

Sara who wa s standing close by answered the baby's question for Gerry. Sara said," Sweet one. When you go to heaven Jesus and his father will provide you with all the gifts you need. Gifts that even Santa can't bring. Gifts that the world does not yet know." Smiling the little girl asked," What kind of gifts?"

Sara replied, " Jesus will paint a smile on your face that will never leave. A smile that will be so bright that when your friends look up to Heaven at night they will see that smile in the stars. He will also let your ears hear the music of angels for all eternity."

Turner walking   over to the little girl taking her from Gerry's arms into his own said," Feel my hug, well Jesus will give you a hug that you will feel long after you are not in his arms. You will feel that hug in your dreams, while you are awake and long after you become an angel."

Gerry then added,' God, our Father will paint rainbows for you, just to say" I love you." He will create warm rain   to kiss your face. He will plant flowers just to say he misses you."

Tiffany added," Sweetie, he will give you laughter that will never end, no more nightmares, no more pain and you will never cry again."

Barrister Frances handing the girl a shining star to put on top of a tree said," Jesus will also give you wonderful memories of your friends   to take with you to Heaven so you are never alone."

Pastor Harry shared," He will also give you a big house where you will always have a family, a family of God's children, a family that will always love you."

Sammy dressed in a red dress started dancing around. " You will be so happy in Heaven that you will dance all the time."

"New Beginnings"

The sick little girl looking at everyone said," I can't wait to go to Heaven now!" The group became somber until Sara walked over and lit up the Christmas fir. " Oh, It looks so pretty!" Tiffany beamed. Everyone feel silent as they became wrapped up in the twinkling lights. " Santa when do we get our gifts?" The sick little tot asked. " Ho, ho, ho, I need my milk and cookies 1st." Gerry laughed. The children ran around to bring cookies to Santa , while Tiffany poured a glass of milk.

" Ho, Ho, Ho." Gerry said laughing as he eat the cookies and drank the milk. The children giggled. " Santa, you have cookie crumbs in your beard." Tiffany smiled. Gerry wiped them off. Gerry then said," Ok, Time to open gifts." All the tots gathered around Gerry. They sat in a circle cross legged on the floor. Gerry sat in a folding chair.

Everyone watched as Gerry passed out the gifts. There were giggles and squeals of joy and delight from the tots as they opened toy trucks, dolls, puzzles, books and lollypops. One reporter and camera man from the local news filmed the happy moment. The reporter also sent out a plea for foster homes for the tots. The tots high on sugar began playing with their new toys.

Tiffany found herself standing in the corner looking at the wee ones wishing she had a baby of he r own. Gerry watched Tiffany. He then broke away from the crowd. He walked over to Tiffany. Gerry still dressed as St. Nick handed Tiffany the homemade pin he made for her. " Merry Christmas." Gerry said with a smile. Surprised Tiffany asked," What is this." " It's just something a made. I know its not fancy but -" Tiffany broke in with a joyful" It's so beautiful. No one has ever made me a gift before."

Tiffany noticed then she and Gerry were standing under the mistletoe. Tiffany shifted her weight from one foot to another. Gerry raised his hand. He touched Tiffany's face gently. Gerry ran his thumb over her lips. He then lightly kissed her. " Do you want to go for a walk?" Gerry asked Tiffany.

" Sure St. Nick, but you should say goodbye to the tots 1st." Tiffany suggested. Gerry gathered the tots to his side. All their little faces were beaming with unspoiled joy. " Ho, Ho, Ho, little ones. I need to be going now. I have lots of toys to deliver tonight. I love you all." Gerry announced. There wa s tears and tight hugs. Finally he tots let St. Nick leave. Tiffany waited a few moments to follow him.

When she did meet Gerry outside of the building he was once again dressed as himself. " Mind Boggling." Tiffany said. " What is?" Gerry asked as he took a step closer toward Tiffany. " This whole night. Is a miracle. Your transformation. Everything." Tiffany said.

" The whole night?" Gerry asked puzzled. " Yes, I know I was the jittled Bride but I was thinking about that also. If he didn't love me enough to show up, well then that was God saving me from a whole heap of unhappiness." Tiffany replied.

Gerry got very quiet at that moment. " Cat got your tongue?" Tiffany asked. Gerry cleared his throat as through he was getting ready to make a speech at the Oscars. " What if Rufus was not a wanker? What if he wanted to be there, but just couldn't be?" Gerry asked. " What are you trying to say?" Tiffany asked.

Gerry pulled out Rufus's letter from his pocket. He slowly handed it over to Tiffany. " What is this?" tiffany asked . Gerry turned as white as a ghost. ' Let's sit down." Gerry said. " You are scaring me." Tiffany responded. Gerry grabbed Tiffany's hand. " Rufus didn't come tonight, not because he didn't love you but because he as you say it died." Gerry reviled. "What! What are you talking about?" Tiffany screamed. " I know this is painful but he's gone." Gerry tried to explain. " What! No! It can't be!" Tiffany said. " I am so sorry." Gerry said.

Tiffany buried her head in Gerry's chest. Crying she asked," How do you know he passed?" Gerry really didn't go into detail. All he said was That he stopped by the toy store and found out. " Is this letter from Rufus?" Tiffany shaking like a leaf asked. Gerry whispered ,"Yes."

" I don't think I can read it." Tiffany cried. " Do you want me to read it to you?" Gerry asked in a gentle tone. Tiffany slowly nodded. Gerry opened the letter. Slowly Gerry read," Dear Tiffany, This is the hardest letter I ever had to write. I am a coward for not being able to speak to you face to face. I would just be broken without you in my life. You are my greatest joy, greatest gift and greatest blessing. How am I supposed to sum up what you have meant to me in a few words? How am I supposed to list the pure moments of joy you have given me? How am I supposed to express my heart's deepest emotion? One word says it all. Love. You have changed my whole world with your love. My whole entire being. At 1st I didn't know who I was or which way to go. I turned one way it wa s two dark. I asked myself 1000s of times wa s it all me? Was my soul dark? I was so confused until I looked ahead and I was able to see you. You are always there. There with the 1st light of your beautiful smile, My enteral dawn to walk the rest of the way on the road to my dreams. You have made ever dream I had come true. But I already know everything I feel is because you love me. As I look back over our time together, I know God sent you my angel and my friend. I will not moan for you and do not moan for me. I will always feel your love surrounding me. "

Tiffany curled up in a ball weeping so hard her clothing became wet. " Its alight Luv, you let it all out." Gerry said. " If I would have known , I would have spent more time with him!" Tiffany cried. " Oh, Luv don't talk like that. Every moment you spent with Rufus enriched his life." Gerry said holding Tiffany. " It wasn't enough time! We were supposed to spend our life together!" Tiffany shouted. " I know sweetheart. I know how much it hurts." Gerry said. " You don't know! You will never understand my pain!' Tiffany crying harder said.

" I do luv. My fiancé died on Christmas day in my arms." Gerry said as he hugged Tiffany tight. Tiffany's whole body stiffed up. Tiffany swallowed hard. " I am so sorry. I had no idea. " Tiffany replied. " Tiffany she was an angel. She illumined a room whenever she walked into it. Angel and that wa s her name, taught me how to pray, love, laugh and believe in the good things ." Gerry shared.

" What happened to her?" Tiffany asked in a soft tone. " It was Christmas Day. We had a family dinner planned. We had just got engaged. Angel had forgotten my Christmas gift at her flat. It wa s just around the block from mine. So Angel went home to get it. I heard her screams. I heard the breaking glass. I heard the car tires squeal. I smelled the smoke of the burning brakes and I saw the face of the drunk driver that ran her over. " Gerry tearfully shared.

Tiffany and Gerry crying hugged one another tightly. Finally when the painful weeping became soft sniffling Gerry said," I was so bitter after Angel died. Don't ever let your light Tiffany be dimmed by bitterness." "How can I go on without Rufus?" Tiffany asked. " God, will lead you Tiffany. If you let me I'll be there also." Gerry said.

" I have to plan his wake. I have to notify friends." Tiffany started rattling off dismal tasks. " Tiffany, I will handle everything." Gerry said. "I couldn't let you do that. You have done so much already." Tiffany objected.

" Please , let me do this for you." Gerry's eyes shining with compassion as those words feel from his lips. Sara suddenly appeared on the sidewalk in front of them. " Some of the babies have been adopted! People are coming from all over to make sure the wee ones have homes!" Sara said excited. Tiffany popped up off the bus bench. " Really?" Tiffany asked happy. " Yes!" Sara's voice filled with pep said. " This is an amazing night!" Tiffany replied.

" Christmas Bells"

Before anyone could say another word, the Abbey's bells rang out joyfully telling the world it was Christmas Day. Sara began to sing," I heard the bells on Christmas Day." Gerry filled with Christmas joy began singing with her.

" What is that? Is that candlelight?" Tiffany said squinting her eyes through the snow. " Yes, it is. Father Harry thought it would be nice for the tots who are not sleeping to hear midnight high mass in the courtyard of the Rose." Sara shared. " What a terrific idea!" Gerry agreed.

" Well let's get back inside, so we don't miss anything." Tiffany said. As the group walked back into The Rose roasted chestnuts peppered the air.   Candlelight illumined   the cold and snowy night.

Bella sang" Silent Night" as the group gathered in the courtyard. Pastor Harry blessed everyone by saying." Everyone created by God is a product of God's love. Some just don't know it yet. Every human being has a primary love language. If when spoken to them opens their hearts and their eyes to why they really exist.   That moment of love, that instance of endearment of recognition and affirmation can open   the hardest of souls. The God of love is in everyone's dna.   The God of hope who came today to earth as a baby to save us all. He who is the bread of life began his ministry hungry and poor. He who is living water was a man who knew thirst.   He prayed, yet he answered your prayers. He wept , yet he dries our tears.   He was sold for 30 sliver pieces, yet he gives us all the treasures in Heaven.   He was lead as a lamb to slaughter , yet he is the good Shepard. He was betrayed by his friends, yet he is the only friend we need. He was abused and his flesh ripped , yet he still heals. He was a man , yet he rose from the dead. He was the king of broken souls , yet he never wore a crown of gold."

With that everyone said," Amen." It was then   Sara who stood in front of the crowd. Holding her lit candle high in the air, Sara said," Just as this candle illumines the darkness, Christ lights up our hearts the moment we accept him. "

After Sara did her little sermon, Turner read the Christmas story form the book of Luke. Everyone listened to it with their hearts not ears.   The service ended with the whole group singing " Joy To The World."

After the morning service, the tots that had been adopted went home with their new parents. The rest of the tots , ten in all went to bed with new hope in their hearts that soon they would be adopted also. Everyone left expect for the staff of The Rose, Bella and Gerry.

Gerry laid awake while everyone slept. Gerry worked all night long. He called on his famous clients, former friends of his family and everyone he could. By morning Gerry owned nothing but the clothing on his back and the belongings in his suitcase.   Gerry had sold everything to raise money to take care of those ten tots who had not been adopted.

That beautiful Christmas morn, Gerry knew he would grant Rufus his dying wish. He would ask Tiffany for her hand after she was done grieving for Rufus. In the morning long before anyone else woke, Gerry began preparing breakfast for everyone.

Tiffany's nose twitched as she inhaled the smell of coffee. Tiffany's eyes fluttered open. A blurry vision of Gerry stood before her. " How did you sleep luv?" Gerry asked in a friendly tone. " last night all feels like a strange dream. Did it really happen?" Tiffany asked. " Yes ,Luv." Gerry replied. " Is Rufus really gone?" Tiffany's eyes filled with sadness. Yes, Sweet. He is gone, but I am here." Gerry said as he reached for he r hand. " I am glad you are here." Tiffany admitted.

Bella awoke then. " Good morning Bella." Tiffany said. " Merry Christmas Morn!" Bella replied in a cheerful tone. But when Bella saw Tiffany's face she knew something w s wrong." What is it? Has Gerry done something to upset you?" Bella asked giving Gerry a death stare. " Last night, I found out that Rufus died. He did not leave me at the altar." Tiffany shared.

" Oh, Honey. I am sorry." Bella said racing over to give Tiffany a hug. Tiffany nearly in tears said," We better get the rest of the crew up." Tiffany did not want to think about Rufus's death. Gerry and Bella talked quietly so they would not upset Tiffany. " Poor girl, her heart must be broken." Bella said. " The memorial service is going to be Monday at the Abbey." Gerry reviled.

" Is there anything, I can do to help?' Bella asked. Gerry got a far off look in his eye. He looked at Tiffany." Just help me get her through her pain." Gerry said. Placing her hand on Gerry's shoulder Bella said," I promise you I will ."

One by one everyone woke up. Gathering at the table for breakfast, Pastor Harry lead everyone in prayer. After Harry said his prayer, Gerry stood up." A god friend of mine once told me that Christmas is about reflection, about looking at your life and having the courage to change. That friend also taught me how to love again, after my fiancé died on a Christmas Day many moons ago now. Yesterday, I sold everything because this amazing friend taught me that material things just don't matter. That the richest man riches is not measured in how big your bank account is or how big your house is. The richest man is mad e rich by how big his heart is, the friends he keeps and by the woman he loves. So wee ones as we speak, I have a crew remolding an old factory. If you let me I like to be your new Da and we can all live there together."

Everyone was so happy and excited. The sick little girl said," Santa heard my prayers, I asked for a new Daddy for Christmas , Now I have one!"

Tiffany whispered in Gerry's ear " Is this for real?" Gerry pulled Tiffany close. " It's all real because you showed me real love. I am in love with you woman. I know you are still hurting for Rufus but-" Tiffany intruded on Gerry's thought with a full on mouth to mouth kiss. " I loved Rufus, but now I know Rufus gifted me with you. That is one gift I will not exchange or try to get a refund on. " With that Gerry kissed her back. Then he said," What do you say? Do you want to be a Mum to these wee ones and be my wife?" " I would be honored." Tiffany replied.

The story of Gerry Cratchit doesn't end there however. Like Old Scrooge, Gerry vowed to honor Christmas in his heart all year long. And Honor he did. He married Tiffany that following Christmas at the Rose. He funded the medical needs for that sick little girl to get well. A wee one who bloomed into a young woman with wee ones of her own. Gerry made amends with Bella . He helped Bella open her own jazz club. It was there she performed until her last days. Gerry and Tiffany transformed London with love and light just as Scrooge did 200 years before them.

Old Rufus sat on his cloud in Heaven smiling. Sara put he r arm around Turner saying." This was the best vacation, I ever had." Turner smiled.

Made in the USA
Lexington, KY
26 November 2014